GW00703163

WE ARE ANIMALS, DON'T FORGET IT

WE ARE ANIMALS, DON'T FORGET IT

Imogen Downes

Published 2021 by Against the Grain Poetry Press
againstthegrainpoetrypress.wordpress.com

ISBN 978-1-9163447-6-1

Printed by 4edge Limited
4edge.co.uk

Contents

For Mr Hoskins, who taught me a love of writing

Imogen's Lament

A fire disguised
as a hero, he came –
a war disguised
as a lover.

The beach was quiet,
but not peaceful.
He was the shadow of the moon;
the knot in the tide.
Was I dipping my toes in
or dragged by the tips of my hair?

He is too full of me
for there to be anything left.

> This space where I once was;
> wash it,
> wash it away,
> hear my song
> evaporate into the wind.

> Tell Procne I'm coming.

> There are so many questions
> I should have asked.

Things I've Thought Long And Hard About And Would Genuinely Like To Know The Answer To

Where did the baby from my Sylvanian Family go?
Does that film we made about a giant evil iguana still exist?
How long does it take to film a series of RuPaul's Drag Race?
When do they film reality TV confessionals?
How do they make it sound like the contestants are talking about the action in real time?
What do my organs look like?
Why am I always bloated?
Do I have any interesting family heritage, or is it really all just Welsh?
Is it possible to build an edible garden like the one in Charlie and the Chocolate Factory?
If it is, has anyone ever done it? If not, why not?
Should I dye my hair?
Why do I get so many spots?
Am I deficient in any vitamins or minerals?
In the final scene of Call Me By Your Name, did Timothée Chalamet really cry like that or did he use eye drops?

Becoming Noah

Prologue

Hell knows all hiding places.
Hell invented them.
That's what makes it Hell.
When the rain comes, and it will,
the sand will not shelter your head.

i.

There was something godly about it.
Something definite
about the way everything started to drip,
how all the good china started to run and
the animals became unusual.
People were pinning bed sheets to the sky
and coughing to hide the rumble.
The sky was painted biblical.

ii.

I dreamt there were waves
lapping at my bedroom window.
We, dry as a strong face,
quietly watched the world rush by.
The flood pulled back into a beast
and lunged at our house –
we're going to die, I thought
we're going to be crushed and drowned –
but the walls didn't quaver
and we held each other madly.

iii.

Once, I ran for the sky without learning to swim
and lost the air.
Now, I pull my socks up every morning
and give a hard stare to the mirror.

iv.

I survived. My family survived.
Everything unfinished died.

Earth

She's wearing her best sweat
as she tugs at your black veil.

Your mouth watering,
ground frothing
globe ash,

your worm womb,
your filthy flour,
your weed ecstasy,

and she is wild,
but you are Mother
and you're letting her toss you around
like a ball pit for the ants,
like the nose powder of a woodlouse,

like it's all roses in the April sun.

Tough as old tree boots.
Soft as a flower bed sheet.

Innocent as a string of dirty pearls.

She will nurse
your ancient flaking skin,
but you'll be the one
to kiss her goodnight.

What Meaningful Question Was Ever Answered Comfortably?

i.
It's the edge, but we think it's nowhere
on this dead-end path we've been following

trying to answer some old question that everybody
has on their lips. We tread the live wire

of horror and excitement when we open our eyes,
taste every answer. They tell us it will be suicide.

We tell them it will be suicide. It's been so long
we can't recognise a love letter when we see one.

ii.
Are we ready to feel every bone
that our fabulous bodies beg us not to?

We Are Animals, Don't Forget It

It's a man's world and we are men so
we flex our God hands and
march to our patches of garden and
we see no mirror, just
chaos waiting to be unraveled, we, who
outwit paradise, who
exceed it with our logic and order, our
dress codes and wifi and borders and
all the other shit we made up because
we had the desire to, because
we're not like other beasts, a
wave breaks in the ocean and we
say *I don't have time for this*, a
flower blooms and we say –
a cloud passes and we say –
a child is born and we say –
a storm unfolds and we say –
the tectonic plates shift beneath our
feet and we slither back to our
immaculate caves to
breathe and piss and gorge and
shit and wank and cry and
fuck and laugh and sleep because
we just can't help ourselves and

outside, the weeds cackle because
they just can't help themselves and

we are pebbles on a
cliff top, hurling ourselves over the edge.

Show Me The Boundary Between You And Everything

when your feet are a worn down carpet
when your head is a curtain rail
when your waist is a tea stained worktop

when you share your legs with a table
and your arms with a chair
and your hair with a toothbrush

when your lungs are rustling branches
and wind swept laundry
and red skied mornings

when there's a pond between your lips
and your hips are heaving walls
when there's a pear tree in your fingers

you are never alone.

Julie and Imogen

Our favourite film is *Call Me By Your Name.*
We talked across half of Asia,
over bánh mì and piping phở,
about how it melted us down –
that perfect story of the human heart
becoming animal with passion,
of throwing yourself into something
with such certainty, to stop
would be to betray every decision
you've ever made. Oh, we talked
through the slats of hostel bunks
and worn coach seat leather
until we became the dense Asian heat
and all we could do was throw
our heads back at the beauty of it.
Julie and Imogen!
Didn't we cry at the end of that film?
Watching the holes unfold on his face
with tears, remembering riding bicycles
through rice fields singing
blessed be the mystery of love…
Like Call Me By Your Name!

Stay Close, Let Go

bowl of miso soup

tray of tempura

pot of soy sauce

six pieces of sushi   rice
prawn   tuna
salmon   octopus   chopsticks
red snapper   pickled ginger
wasabi paste

This time last year I was on a night flight to Japan
trying to watch that film about
billboards and Missouri,
glugging pints of juice from a tiny cup,
flying away from everyone I'd ever known.
A brave sakura, bursting my petals before last frost.

I wasn't thinking about me now

eating a Japanese takeaway to reminisce.
The food doesn't look the same.
I don't have the right bowls.
The plates are faded.
The tray is too small.

This is a celebration.

I like to mark anniversaries with eulogies.
Often, I don't want to let go
but now I must remember that bravery
is
the   most

real   thing
I   can
hold
on to.

I Wonder What The Birds Make Of Us

Their opinions of humans and scarecrows
are much the same.
So other than something to be avoided,
probably nothing at all.

That's the thing about birds;
they don't romanticise themselves.
They don't use other creatures as longing metaphors for freedom.
They don't tether themselves to their boundaries.
They're not up there wondering what we make of them.

To Talk About You Without Using Your Name

would be to insult
the breathless pull of the world
and the words
we swirl on our brushes
as we begin to paint.

Your name
is stitched
into the skeleton
of everything.
It is your title.
Your summary.
Your loyalty.
It is what your mother
thought of when
she first saw you.

Your name
is what the horizon
was drawn to hold,
the smoke
was blown to spell,
the water
was poured to gush.

Your name
is a phoenix
taking flight
from a tongue.

Your name,
Tom Dewey,
your name.

We are a part of the waterfall
Giggling rainbow arched between us
Queasy with caffeine high

and right then
dusk was morning
noon was dawn
we too unfurled at the base of that waterfall
our skin, unexpected
our limbs, elsewhere
water on water on
water on
water
if I had cried it
would have just been part of the fall
I howled like a wild thing
rolled my tongue out to
show the world my insides
there were no words
just a zoo in my throat cut loose
I leapt over rocks towards
the heavy breast of a fluid universe
yelled in a stirring language
we are the same thing

The First Time I Saw A Woman Masturbate Outside Of Porn

there was no performance.
No hurling of hot screams,
no thrusting plastic body parts at the lens,
no demanding me to fuck her,
harder, faster, bigger,
stretch me open until there's nothing left
but a gaping hole of your desire.

Just Amber
and the serene joy she gifted herself.
And me, on our communal throne,
celebrating with her.

21

Adele has an album called *21*.
All of her albums are named
after the age she was
when she released them.
Rolling in the Deep,
Set Fire to the Rain
and *Someone Like You*
all appear on *21*.

Shit.

On my 21st birthday,
I woke up in a beach front cabin in Thailand.
It'd been planned for months –
an ultimate blow out for the big two one.
There'd be sunrise strolls along the sand,
paddle-boarding in the diamond waves,
bubbly jacuzzi baths and poolside pina coladas.
It was going to be perfection.

It was going to be

      perfection.

When I got there I expectantly
waited for euphoria to kick in.
I waited
and waited
and incessantly noticed each grain of sand
out of place,
each wave too salty.

I've been told this is the prime of my life
and I couldn't complain if it was.
But I hope they're wrong,

and that I will mature in richness
like a wine or cheese, or a tree;
that my prime will not be raucous hedonism,
but quiet wisdom.

Some people tell me
I will lose hope
as I get older.
Some also say you
grow to be more peaceful.

Maybe the two go hand in hand.

I Don't Need To Dream Anymore

The whole world:

oceans and roads
wind and bones

animals and reason
mountains and motion

words and coal
a cave and a soul

death and sex
stories and breath

It's all here,
inside me.

Thank You

Thank you Thank you Thank you Tom Thank you for making me songs and singing them to me even though you feel embarrassed to sing Thank you for making me a game about how much you love me Thank you for leaving me a smiley face plate of fruit on your pillow Thank you for buying me thoughtful gifts Thank you for my star map Thank you for the book you made me Thank you for my poems Thank you for walking miles to see me Thank you for telling me that everything is going to be okay Thank you for listening Thank you for telling me you love me Thank you for loving me Thank you for dressing up with me Thank you for taking down the tent when I was messing around Thank you for buying me food Thank you for almost going ice skating with me Thank you for coming to my gigs Thank you for admiring my creativity Thank you for being my hype man Thank you for being kind to my family Thank you for smiling Thank you for looking after yourself Thank you for pouring your poetry into the world Thank you for staying humble Thank you for crying in front of me Thank you for introducing me to your family Thank you for introducing me to your friends Thank you for dancing like you didn't give a fuck Thank you for saying you'll drink less Thank you for saying sorry Thank you for bringing me breakfast in bed Thank you for cooking me breakfast Thank you for wanting to understand my body Thank you for taking the time to understand my body Thank you for loving in a way that allows me to be free Thank you for being honest with me Thank you for calling me Thank you for asking me out Thank you for laughing Thank you for taking me to see Queen Thank you for the spontaneity Thank you for buying me flowers Thank you for showing my writing to your family Thank you for my card when I got the job Thank you for being proud of me I am proud of you Thank you for loving our love Thank you for loving loving me Thank you for running me baths Thank you for washing me Thank you for offering to take the sanitary towel out of my pants Thank you for calling my doctor Thank you for watching shit telly with me even though you only like good telly Thank you for helping me write those poems Thank you for carrying my bag when my back is sore Thank you for getting up early with me on your days off Thank you for all the sleepovers Thank you for changing your bed sheets
you should change them more often

I See Myself For The First Time Again

I drop seeds wherever I go.
Throw spring on the ground and watch new life
grow from the scrapings of my pockets.
There are daffodils in my handbag,
a nest of chicks behind my ear,
cherry blossom in the bottom
of my chest of drawers.
Even when winter clings to my ribs I pull
garlands from my lips and find
solace in the elbow of a speckled egg.

Wherever I go, people dance.
Wherever I step, flowers bloom.
If there is a tree, I will climb it,
command fruit from its branches.

Leaves grow. Rivers thaw and flow.
Pregnant women leave their clothes
and follow me.

The world appears to gently
burst through its own skin.

Acknowledgements

The poem *Imogen's Lament* is inspired by the play *The Love Of The Nightingale* by Timberlake Wertenbaker; *I See Myself For The First Time Again* is inspired by the painting *Primavera* by Sandro Botticelli.

Thank you Grandad, who read early drafts of these poems, and Dad – your support has been unparalleled.

Thank you Tom, who has provided great inspiration and feedback.

Thank you Sarah Forbes, Jess Mookherjee, Karen Dennison and Abegail Morley.

Thank you to my wonderful family. You're the best.

Imogen Downes is a Bristolian poet and theatre-maker. She has worked with Bristol Old Vic and Cheltenham Literature Festival, and was named on *Rife Magazine's* 24 Under 24 list in 2018 for her work in poetry. *We Are Animals, Don't Forget It* is her debut pamphlet.

'Imogen Downes's voice is fresh and energetic as she writes about her relationship to the world – how she inhabits it and is inhabited by it. She is a poet who questions, both directly and indirectly, as she searches for answers. Here are poems about love, a favourite film, the singer Adele, the female body, a Japanese meal, culminating in an affirmation of herself and the world. *We Are Animals, Don't Forget It* is an exciting debut from a poet to watch.'

- Mara Bergman

'These are hungry poems, always stretching themselves to evoke huge feelings. Downes writes strikingly and well. At her best, her intensity becomes her subject and she shows us what it is to live and feel in absolutes. Her poems are interested in the spiritual but also remote from it, poised between the desire to transcend the self and the proud egotism of strong emotion. The effect is invigorating. I read this pamphlet from cover to cover without effort and came away thinking: what a fine and terrible thing to be alive.'

- Tom Sastry

N F 9 · 40
AM
£5·99P

'This collection moved me – through its depths, layers and explorations of our shared human experiences alongside the nuances of a single life. Making sense of the existence of God, nature, the beauty of art, sushi, romance and friendship. *We Are Animals, Don't Forget It* examines the many ways love speaks, and how to really listen when it does.'

- Rebecca Tantony

ISBN 978-1-9163447-6-1

£6.00